WARRIOR LORE

Previously published in the same series:

Lord Peter and Little Kerstin

Warrior Lore

Ian Cumpstey

Northern Displayers, Skadi Press

Warrior Lore

Published in 2014 by Northern Displayers, Skadi Press, England
www.northerndisplayers.co.uk

ISBN 978-0-9576120-1-3

Contents

Preface

The Scandinavian folk ballads translated here are narrative songs, and as such they represent part of a strong storytelling tradition, combining a plot with poetry and music. Ballads of this type were first written down in about the sixteenth century, although they may have been sung centuries earlier. The ballads in this second volume are rather different in style from those included in my previous collection, *Lord Peter and Little Kerstin*. One difference is that the characters, or character names, Lord Peter and Little Kerstin do not appear. Also, supernatural beings are less prominent — elves, necks, and mermaids are completely absent, although we do encounter some trolls. The subject matter in this collection, then, is more focussed on fighter-songs, warrior-ballads, and heroes' tales.

While Lord Peter and Little Kerstin seem to be rather generic character names, appearing as they do in diverse roles in unrelated storylines, the characters in this collection occupy their own much more well-defined places in their own stories.

Several of the characters appear in the poetic Edda. The story of Thor-karl's hammer, *The Hammer Hunt*, with Locke Leve, Trolletram, and Freijenborg, is unmistakably a rendition of the poem known as *Thrymskvida*. Diderick of Bern, Sivar Snare Sven, and Widrick Waylandsson are warriors well-known from north European literature. They appear here in the ballads of *Widrick Waylands-*

son's Fight with Long-Ben Reyser and the *Twelve Strong Fighters* (and also in several other related folk-ballads), and they also feature in the Edda. In *Widrick Waylandsson's Fight with Long-Ben Reyser*, Widrick mentions his parents, Wayland the smith and Bodil, a King's daughter. The story of the encounter of these two (i.e., Völund and Bödvild) is told in *Völundarkvida*. Sivar Snare Sven (i.e., Sigurd Fafnirsbane) is central to the hero poems of the Edda, while King Diderick appears there transiently.

The ballads of *Sir Hjalmar*, and of Hilla and Hillebrand in *Hilla-Lill*, offer variations on the theme of the warrior who, after falling for the "wrong" girl (or at least being the wrong guy), dispatches her kinsmen (her father — the King — and brothers), and who meets his own fate at the hands of a surviving brother. *Sven Swan-White*, a fighter who is particularly keen on riddles, and the (in Sweden unnamed) *Stablemates* also have ballads all their own.

Some of the other characters are more or less well-known historical figures. The ballad of the the princess Elin and Sir Sune Folkesson and *The Cloister Raid* at Vreta tells a story from history, of Swedish early royalty from the 1200s. Harald Hardrada was a Norwegian King; the story of his contest with Heming, told here in *Heming and King Harald*, also appears in the Icelandic Flatey book manuscript as *The Story of Heming Aslacksson*. But this story seems to be one of poetic literature rather than of history; in fact, Harald is known to have been killed not at the hands of Heming, but at Stamford Bridge in England in 1066. Another story about Heming is told in *Heming and the Mountain Troll*, but little else is known about him.

The form of the verse also deserves some comment. Previously we have seen two-line rhyming verses separated by chorus (*omkväde*) lines. This verse form is also seen in this collection. But much more common here is a four-line verse format in which the second and fourth lines rhyme (ABCB), which may or may not be followed by a chorus (*omkväde*) line or lines. The ballad Sven Swan-White is different: there the four-line verses are made up of two pairs of rhyming couplets (AABB), and there is no *omkväde* line. Although the rhyming patterns are clear, the rhymes are not always perfect in the Swedish originals.

Most of this collection is based on the Swedish tradition, but I have also included one ballad, *Heming and King Harald*, from the Norwegian.

It should be straightforward for English readers to make a simple pronunciation of most of the (Swedish) names in this book. But a couple of points require an explanation. The final "e" in names such as *Sune, Locke, Leve, Snare,* and *Folke* is pronounced as a final unstressed syllable (as in *sooner, locker*, etc.). Note, though, that the "Dane" in *Holger Dane* is an English epithet referring to his country of origin, so it is pronounced as in English. The "E" as the first syllable in *Elin* is pronounced similarly to the first syllable of *ailing* or *apex*. The first "e" in *Leve* is pronounced in the same way, so *Leve* is pronounced similarly to the name of the Australian tennis player. Finally, "j" is pronounced as "y" in *Freijenborg* and *Hjalmar*.

Preface

1   Widrick Waylandsson's Fight with Long-Ben Reyser

These first two ballads concern the legendary heroes of northern
Europe, Diderick of Bern and Sivar Snare Sven (sometimes called
Sigurd). These heroes were known from songs and stories through-
out the Germanic regions, and their status was like that of Arthur
in Britain or Charlemagne in the south. The greatest of King Diderick's ever-winning fighters was Widrick Waylandsson, the son of
Wayland the smith.

The ballads *Widrick Waylandsson's fight with Long-Ben Reyser*
and *Twelve Strong Fighters* are found as separate entities in the
Swedish tradition, but they represent the first and second halves of
a longer story that has been recorded as a single ballad in Denmark.

The first part begins with Diderick and his men at his home
castle in Bern (or Hall). As Diderick ponders his invincibility, one
of his men, Bernard Wifaring, suggests that King Isingen of Bortingsburgh could be a challenging opponent. Diderick does not ap-
preciate the lack of confidence, or the suggestion that he may not
be world number one, but he nevertheless agrees to go off to Bortingsburgh to fight Isingen, and suggests that doubting Bernard lead
the way as flag-bearer. Bernard declines this offer as he is afraid
of a troll, Long-Ben Reyser (whose name means the long-legged

troll or giant), who lives in the woods on the way to Bortingsburgh. Widrick Waylandsson volunteers to ride first to take care of the troll, and this he does. The first ballad ends with Widrick playing a joke on his companions. He pretends to have been injured by Long-Ben Reyser, and laughs when they are then afraid to see the corpse of the troll.

King Diderick he sat in Bern,
  And he gazed out so wide:
"I never knew a fighter,
  "Who'd challenge me to fight."
There stands a castle at Bern,
  And there lives King Diderick.

Answered Bernard Wifaring,
  He'd travelled far and wide:
"There is a fighter in Bortingsburgh,
  "Who you'd not dare to fight."

King Diderick took him by the throat,
  And then took out his knife:
"You'll show me who that fighter is,
  "Or it'll cost your life."

"Isingen is that King's name,
  "He rules over castles and forts,
"And Sivard is his flag-bearer,
  "He never came off his horse."

"Listen, Bernard Wifaring,
  "You've wandered far and wide,
"You shall carry my flag today,
  "And foremost shall you ride."

2

"I don't deserve that honour,
  "My master's flag to bear.
"There is a troll in Bortingen's wood,
  "It's big and strong, I fear."

Answered Widrick Waylandsson,
  A fighter brave and good:
"Then let me be the first man,
  "To ride in Bortingen's wood."

Widrick he leapt onto Shymbling's back,
  His spear held at his knee:
"If I'm not back by evening time,
  "You needn't wait for me."

It was Widrick Waylandsson,
  Rode through the woods awhile.
He came to Long-Ben Reyser,
  Who lay there black and vile.

And it was Widrick Waylandsson,
  Hit Long-Ben where he lay:
"Get up now, Long-Ben Reyser,
  "I'll talk with you today!"

"Here have I lain for fifteen years,
  "All on my left-hand side,
"And never has a fighter come,
  "To challenge me to fight.

"Ride on, ride on, little man,
  "And put away your spear.
"It doesn't suit a stable boy,
  "To challenge a fighter fierce."

Here have I lain for fifteen years, all on my left-hand side.

"I am not a stable boy,
  "Although you thought it right,
"But rather has that fighter come,
  "Who'll challenge you to fight."

And it was Long-Ben Reyser,
  He lifted up his ear:
"Tell me then, my fair young swain,
  "Of your blunt weapons here."

"Shymbling is my noble horse,
  "Born of Grimmer's stud,
"And Mimmering is my good sword,
  "Hard with fighters' blood.

"Skrepping is my glorious shield,
  "That many swords has shattered,
"Blank my proud and shining helm,
  "That many arrows scattered.

"Wayland is my father's name,
  "He was a smith so fine,
"And Bodil is my mother's name,
  "Fair daughter of a King.

"And I am Widrick Waylandsson,
  "In iron I am dressed,
"And this I'll say to you in truth,
  "As a fighter, I'm the best!"

"And well I know then Mimmering,
  "Your nasty rusty sword,
"And also half-legged Shymbling,
  "Your old out-ridden horse."

Shymbling sprang with both his legs,
    Fell onto Reyser's side,
And so he broke his seven ribs,
    And they began to fight.

It was Long-Ben Reyser,
    He swung his staff around,
He swung for Widrick Waylandsson,
    But his staff sank into the ground.

And it was Long-Ben Reyser,
    Began to moan and stammer:
"My staff is stuck fast in the earth,
    "Like it was hit with a hammer."

Widrick was wary and Shymbling ready,
    And Widrick's sword was drawn.
He severed Reyser's finger off,
    And then another one.

"I'll cut you up, Reyser, so small,
    "Like leaves blown through the mud,
"If you don't show me your red gold,
    "That you have in this wood."

"Now listen up, my fair young swain,
    "If you take me alive,
"All the gold I've ever owned,
    "All this to you I'll give."

Widrick rode and Reyser crawled,
    And both were the same height,
And soon they came to a well-built house,
    Its golden roof shone bright.

"Listen, Widrick Waylandsson,
    "Climb down now from your horse,
"And lift that stone that blocks the door,
    "To reach my golden stores."

Widrick tried with all his might,
    The stone he couldn't shift.
Reyser took it with finger and thumb,
    So light for him to lift.

"Listen up, my fair young man,
    "You have a name so grand,
"But stronger am I with my fingers two,
    "Than you with both your hands."

Answered Widrick Waylandsson,
    He didn't like his tone:
"A court-man true I never knew,
    "To waste his strength on stones."

And it was Widrick Waylandsson,
    His sword drawn from his side,
And he cut Long-Ben Reyser down,
    So at his feet he died.

And then he took the dead man's blood,
    He smeared it on his horse.
He rode back to King Diderick,
    And said he was wounded sore.

"Have you been hit, have you been hurt,
    "By Reyser? This is grave.
"We'll go back then to Bern again,
    "No more out here we'll play."

And it was Widrick Waylandsson,
Began to smile instead:
"How will you fight with living men,
"If you dare not face the dead?"

"If you have beaten Reyser,
"It's said in the land so wide,
"Then there's no fighter in the world,
"Who'd challenge you to fight."
There stands a castle at Bern,
And there lives King Diderick.

2 | Twelve Strong Fighters

This ballad follows on from *Widrick Waylandsson's Fight with Long-Ben Reyser*. This second part of the story begins with the arrival of Diderick and his men at Isingen's castle at Bortingsburgh. There is a run-down of the party of twelve (they may be a larger number in total — seventy-seven is the poet's "estimate"), with descriptions of their shield-arms and characteristics. Isingen sends out his man, Sivar, to challenge one of Diderick's fighters. A young boy, Hamerlen is chosen, and he borrows Widrick Waylandsson's champion horse, Shymbling, for the jousting session. Hamerlen loses the tournament, but when he tells Sivar his name, Sivar realises that the boy is his nephew. He takes pity on him and lets him keep his horse. So Hamerlen returns to his companions to tell them that he has beaten Sivar and tied him up. This they take for a joke, and Widrick, who despite his own previous form, apparently can't stand a joke, goes to investigate. Sivar is forced to escape, and he returns to King Isingen at Bortingsburgh castle with only an oak tree to show for his troubles.

They were seven and seventy,
  When out from Hall they went,
And when they came to Bortingsburgh,
  They pitched their silken tents.
  It thunders under the fierce court-men,
  when they ride.

King Isingen stood in Bortingsburgh,
  And he looked out so wide,
And he saw twelve strong fighters,
  Outside the castle ride.

"Listen, Sivar Snare Sven,
  "To what I say to you:
"Go and see those fighters' shields,
  "Down to the tents you'll go."

It was Sivar Snare Sven,
  Down to the tents he rode:
"Before we ride a joust today,
  "Your shields to me you'll show."

There shone out from the first shield,
  A lion grand and fine,
And so a crown of reddest gold,
  It is King Diderick's sign.

There shone out from the second shield,
  A hammer and a tong.
That carried Widrick Waylandsson,
  He strikes and captures none.

There shone out from the third shield,
  A pair of gilded spurs.
That carried young Sir Hamerlen,
  He's always riding first.

There shone out from the fourth shield,
A dragon, wild in flight.
Carried by Orm Ungersven,
He's not afraid to fight.

There shone out from the fifth shield,
A kettle made of copper.
That carried Monk Sir Alvar,
Who fighters like to follow.

There shone out from the sixth shield,
A gaming-board of gold.
That carried Hillevan Hakonsson,
A hero to behold.

There shone out from the seventh shield,
A fiddle and a bow.
That carried Folke the fiddler,
He'll drink and never doze.

There shone out from the eighth shield,
A wolf, and it was strong.
Carried by young Ulf from Jern,
To take revenge he longs.

There shone out from the ninth shield,
A dragon, it was red.
Carried by young Holger Dane,
He's killed so many dead.

There shone out from the tenth shield,
A falcon, it was white.
That carried Master Hillebrand,
He always wants to fight.

There shone out from the eleventh shield,
 Three arrows, silver-bright.
That carried Bernard Wifaring,
 On him fighters rely.

There shone out from the twelfth shield,
 A raven, all in brown.
That carried Richard Ravengarth,
 For rhymes and runes he's known.

"Which of you fierce fighters,
 "The best can ride a course?
"Against him I will joust today,
 "For saddle and for horse.

"Which of you King's court-men,
 "Against me dares to ride?
"You shouldn't then delay too long,
 "But meet me soon outside."

They cast their dice on the gaming board,
 The dice they rolled so wide,
They fell to young Sir Hamerlen,
 Against Sivar he'd ride.

They cast their dice on the gaming board,
 The dice they tumbled so,
And it was young Sir Hamerlen,
 To the riding ground he'd go.

Up stood young Sir Hamerlen,
 All round the hall he'd been,
And up he went to the high loft,
 To Widrick Waylandsson in.

"Listen, Widrick Waylandsson,
  "We're both on the same side.
"So lend me Shymbling for today,
  "A joust I have to ride."

"Sivar is a half-blind man,
  "Can't see his lance's end.
"If Shymbling's wounded while you ride,
  "You'll never make amends."

"My fifteen castles in Bortingsland,
  "I'll set as guarantee.
"If Shymbling's wounded while I ride,
  "All these you'll get from me."

"You'll not get Shymbling then today,
  "Still more I would demand:
"All your castles in Bortingsland,
  "And your youngest sister's hand."

"My castles up in Bortingsland,
  "I'll set as guarantee.
"My youngest sister's hand you'll have,
  "And my own neck from me."

Hamerlen jumped onto Shymbling's back,
  So gladly did he ride,
And Shymbling thought it curious,
  To feel a spur in his side.

Hamerlen's golden helm shone bright,
  Like the sun at midsummerstide:
"Lord God have mercy on me, poor boy,
  "When against Sivar I ride!"

And so they rode the first joust, they rode with spirits high.

And so they rode the first joust,
    They rode with spirits high,
And broken snapped their shield-straps,
    So great their horses' might.

And so they rode the second joust,
    They were two fighters strong,
And off came Hamerlen's saddle-ring,
    And downward he was flung.

"Now listen up, my fair young swain,
    "For some time more we'll ride.
"You'd better fix your horse's girth,
    "It's hanging to one side."

And so they rode the third joust,
    And Sivar was enraged,
For it was young Sir Hamerlen,
    Far from his line he strayed.

His sword it shone in Sivar's hand,
    As round he rode in spurs:
"You watch yourself, my fair young swain,
    "You'll never finish first.

"I've beaten you now to the ground,
    "And now your horse I've won,
"So tell me now, my fair young swain,
    "From whereabouts you've come.

"I've beaten you now to the ground,
    "And now your horse is mine,
"So tell me soon and don't delay,
    "Your name and your father's line."

"My father is King Abelom,
  "He lives in Bortingsland,
"And I am young Sir Hamerlen,
  "As I ride through the land."

"Your father is he King Abelom,
  "And your mother's royal too?
"Well then you are my sister's son,
  "I see I know you now.

"Your father is he King Abelom?
  "Then we're on the same side.
"I didn't know you earlier,
  "So keep your horse and ride.

"You take both of our shield-straps,
  "And tie me to a tree,
"And ride back to the fighters tents,
  "And say you've beaten me."

And so he took their shield-straps,
  And bound him to an oak,
And he rode back to the fighters tents,
  To tell the fighter-folk.

In came young Sir Hamerlen,
  Cast down his sword and spoke:
"I've beaten Sivar Snare Sven,
  "And bound him to an oak."

"Listen up, young Hamerlen,
  "This has to be a joke.
"With Sivar's blessing was it done,
  "If you bound him to an oak."

Widrick he was a serious man,
  A jest he couldn't stand.
He climbed onto a little horse,
  To ride into the land.

And it was Sivar Snare Sven,
  Saw Widrick Waylandsson ride.
He pulled the oak up by its roots,
  As bound he couldn't fight.

King Isingen stood in Bortingsburgh,
  He looked out into the land,
And he saw Sivar Snare Sven,
  A great flower in his hands.

Sivar he came back to Bortingsburgh,
  The oak tree in his hands:
"Now you see, my Lord and King,
  "A gift from my dear friends."
It thunders under the fierce court-men,
  when they ride.

He lifted me up and we rode away.

3   Hilla-Lill

This ballad tells the story of Hilla and Hillebrand. The story is told
in the first person by Hilla, who is speaking to the Queen in whose
court she is living. She tells of how as a princess she fell in love
with a knight at her father's court, and how they ran away together.
Her father the King and her seven brothers came in pursuit. A key
point of this story is the belief in keeping a warrior's name secret in
a fight. Hillebrand asks Hilla not to call him by name, but after he
has killed her father and six of the brothers, she calls out to him,
by name, to spare her youngest brother. Hillebrand is killed, and
Hilla is roughly taken home by her surviving brother and punished.
After Hilla has finished telling her story to the Queen, she dies, and
the ballad ends.

A very similar and yet clearly distinct ballad is also known that
tells an alternative story of Hilla and Hillebrand. In that version
of the story, when they ride away from the King's court, Hilla is
disguised as a servant boy. Hillebrand again recieves his fatal bane-
wounds after Hilla cries out his name in a fight against her father's
men, who have been in pursuit. But in that ballad, Hillebrand does
not die immediately, but is able to ride home wounded, taking Hilla
with him. They ride through the 30-mile forest without speaking,
and eventually Hillebrand dies at his father's home.

Miss Hilla-lill sat in her chamber and sewed,
  Who knows my sorrow but God,
She knitted with silk and embroidered with gold.
  He never lives, who I should tell of my sorrow.

And quickly the message came in to the Queen,
  "Miss Hilla-lill's sewing so wild in her seams."

The Queen she stepped through the door inside,
  And Hilla-lill saw her with gentle eyes.

The Queen hit Hilla-lill's flower-cheek bright:
  "Why are you sewing so wildly tonight?"

"My gracious Queen, don't punish me so,
  "I'm a King's daughter, as you may know."

And Hilla-lill patted the pillows so blue:
  "Sit here, my Queen, and rest awhile, do.

"My gracious lady, Oh, sit here with me,
  "And I'll tell you all of my sorrow and grief:"

While I was still in my dear father's yard,
  Over me daily his knights stood guard.

One of them was Sir Hillebrand,
  The son of the King of Engeland.

And it was young Sir Hillebrand,
  I fled with him from my father's land.

Hillebrand saddled his palfrey grey,
  He lifted me up and we rode away.

And when we had come to the rosy hills,
  There Hillebrand wanted to rest for a while.

He rested his eyes and he lay by my knee,
And slumbered and slept there, so lovely and sweet.

"Hillebrand, Hillebrand, don't sleep here,
"My father and seven brothers are near.

"Oh, Hillebrand, Hillebrand, wake I pray,
"I hear my father's palfrey grey."

"When I ride out into battle today,
"Hilla-lill, Hilla, don't mention my name."

In the first fight of the battle he slew,
My father and six of my brothers, too.

He met in the second skirmish there,
My youngest brother with gold-yellow hair.

"Oh, Hillebrand, Hillebrand, still your sword,
" My brother should not have this death in store."

No sooner than I had spoken these words,
With seven wounds Hillebrand fell to the earth.

Hillebrand stroked his red-bloody sword,
"If you weren't Hilla, you'd have this in store."

My brother took hold of my gold-yellow hair,
He knotted it fast to his saddle there.

So quickly he rode, and I had to run,
And I was so badly wounded then.

Never was there so little a root,
It didn't trip and scratch my foot.

And never was there so little a stone,
It didn't scrape the skin from my bone.

And when we had come to the castle gate,
  My sorrowful mother was standing in wait.

My brother he wanted to have me killed,
  My mother she wanted to have me sold.

And so I was sold for a bell so new,
  It hangs in the church of St Mary now.

My mother she heard the chime of the bell,
  And broken her heart into pieces fell.

When Hilla-lill all of her piece had said,
  There she fell in the Queen's arms dead.

The Queen she got such a terrible fright,
  Who knows my sorrow but God,
When Hilla-lill died in her arms that night.
  He never lives, who I should tell of my sorrow.

4 | Sir Hjalmar

This ballad bears certain similarities to the previous one. Again, a knight at the court, Sir Hjalmar, falls in love with the King's daughter. He kills the King, and fights the girl's seven brothers. After killing six of the brothers, he spares the youngest. But the youngest brother does not show his appreciation — he kills Sir Hjalmar, and when he goes to tell his sister, she, in turn, kills him. Thus she is left as the sole survivor, having lost her father, her seven brothers, and her lover.

Sir Hjalmar he served in the royal court,
> For forty weeks and three years more.
> *So handsome rode Hjalmar upon his horse.*

For no other prize did he serve there,
> Than the King's own daughter, for she was so fair.

And quickly word came in to the King:
> "Sir Hjalmar he's trying your daughter to win."

The King he spoke to his small boys two:
> "You fetch that Hjalmar in to me."

And Hjalmar he stepped through the door inside,
　　The King he saw him with furious eyes.

"Sir Hjalmar, hear what I have to say:
　　"What can you have to my daughter to say?"

The King he spoke in an angry mood:
　　"You'll pay for this with your heart-blood."

And not a thing the King he knew,
　　But off his head and his right hand flew.

Sir Hjalmar he went to the maiden to speak:
　　"If you've any counsel, then give it to me."

"I'll give you counsel the best that I can,
　　"You saddle your horse and ride from the land."

"The ladies and maidens would wonder and cry,
　　"If I should escape and shamefully fly."

Sir Hjalmar he rode to the rosy ground,
　　And with him he took his hawk and hound.

Sir Hjalmar he rode to the rosy woods,
　　And there met her seven brothers good.

"Sir Hjalmar, Sir Hjalmar, don't come too near,
　　"We don't hold you in our hearts so dear.

"You've killed our father and paid us no fee,
　　"You've tempted our sister, and angry are we."

"Seven gold chests I've collected in store,
　　"Take these as a fee for that father of yours."

"We'll take no other fee today:
　　"Your hand and your head we'll take away."

And he met her seven brothers good.

"Before I let my heart-blood flow,
"So I shall fight you freely now."

Sir Hjalmar he swung his horse around,
And six of the brothers he cut to the ground.

Sir Lars he begged as he fell to his knees:
"Sir Hjalmar, Sir Hjalmar, Oh, spare me please!"

Sir Hjalmar rode first with his hair blowing free,
Sir Lars rode behind him as bad as can be.

And not a thing Sir Hjalmar he knew,
But off his head and his right hand flew.

Sir Lars set the head on a gilded spear,
He rode away to his sister's bower.

"Good day, good day, O sister of mine,
"Here is the head of your dear man."

"You've brought me the head of my dear man?
"Come into my bower for mead and wine."

The first drink from the cup that he drank,
A silver-blade knife in his heart she sank.

The maiden she danced in her purple shoes,
But soon she cried in her sorrowful mood.

"My brothers are lying for ravens and hounds,
"And now I shall bury my man in the ground."
So handsome rode Hjalmar upon his horse.

5 | The Hammer Hunt

This ballad is unusual or even unique in the documented Scandinavian folk-tradition in that it has as its subject matter the Æsir gods of old Norse myth. The story it tells, of the quest to fetch home Thor's lost hammer, is well-known from the poetic Edda, where it is known as *The Song of Thrym*. The story of the folk-ballad closely follows the classically known plot. The names are altered somewhat from how they are known in the Edda, but they are unmistakable. Thus, Thor becomes *Thor-karl*, Freya is *Freijenborg*, Loki is *Locke Leve*, and Thrym the troll is *Troll-tram*.

After he discovers that his hammer is missing, Thor-karl sends Locke Leve out to find it, starting at the home of the prime suspect, Troll-tram. So Locke Leve flies off (for fly he can) and confronts Troll-tram, who makes no secret of the fact that he has stolen the hammer, and demands the hand of Freijenborg in marriage before the hammer will be returned. When Locke Leve tells Thor-karl and Freijenborg this back in Asagard, they are not best pleased, but Thor-karl decides that he will dress as a bride and go to Troll-tram in Freijenborg's place. At the wedding feast, the hammer is brought out, and Thor-karl is able to retrieve it and to strike down the trolls.

Thor-karl sat high in his seat,
　　Thinking of where he'd gone:
"Troll-tram stole my hammer of gold,
　　"I should never have gone!
Thor-karl trains his foals with reins.

"Listen, Locke Leve,
　　"Servant-boy of mine,
"Go and fly the land around,
　　"And find that hammer of mine."

And it was Locke Leve,
　　He made himself gold-wings.
He flew down into Troll-tram's yard,
　　Where Troll-tram stood and smithed.

"What's the news from Asagard,
　　"The land from where you've passed?
"Running you came with strides so long,
　　"Flying here so fast."

"Here's the news from Asagard,
　　"All's dark and nothing's fine:
"Thor-karl's lost his hammer of gold,
　　"That's what I've come to find.

"Listen up, old Trolle-tram,
　　"To what I say to you:
"Did you take Thor-karl's hammer?
　　"Don't hide it from me now!"

"I've taken Thor-karl's hammer,
　　"I wouldn't hide a word,
"For fifteen fathoms and forty,
　　"It lies under the earth.

Where Troll-tram stood and smithed.

"Now give Thor-karl my answer,
　"His hammer he'll not get,
"Until I have Miss Freijenborg,
　"The sunbeam fair to wed."

Locke Leve took his wings,
　And through the air he sped,
And landed back in Asagard,
　As Thor-karl went to bed.

"Troll-tram sends an answer:
　"Your hammer you'll not get,
"Until he has Miss Freijenborg,
　"The sunbeam fair to wed."

And it was fair Miss Freijenborg,
　So angry when she heard,
From every finger, blood burst out,
　And ran down to the earth.

"Listen, dearest sister,
　"To what I say to you:
"How much gold would you give to me,
　"To be that bride for you?"

And so it was Thor-karl himself,
　A wedding-dress he made,
And off he went to Troll-tram's yard,
　Where he would be a bride.

And so it was old Trolle-tram,
　The bride he soon did see:
"So fetch me in my finest clothes,
　"And dress me handsomely."

A roasted ox the bride ate up,
  And fifteen tubs of oats,
And all the bread that had been baked,
  And two big pans of sprouts.

And fifteen salmon she ate up,
  And lots of little fish,
The bride she'd had her greatest meal,
  But now for a drink she wished.

"Listen up, old Trolle-tram,
  "This is a wedding here,
"So throw away those beakers small,
  "And bring us buckets of beer!"

Old Trolle-tram he answered,
  High in his hall he sat:
"I've never seen so small a bride,
  "Eat as much as that!"

And Locke Leve answered,
  He hoped to win some praise:
"She's longed so much to be with you,
  "She's fasted fourteen days."

And so it was old Trolle-tram,
  Was pleased by what was said,
And Thor-karl's hammer was soon brought in,
  And on the table set.

Fifteen were the small-trolls,
  Who bore the hammer in.
The bride she took it with just one hand,
  And grasped it under her skin.

And so it was the young bride,
　　Across the table strode,
And struck out at old Trolle-tram,
　　So at her feet he died.

And so it was the young bride,
　　Began to go around,
And fifteen trolls and forty,
　　She laid out on the ground.
Thor-karl trains his foals with reins.

6   The Stablemates

This ballad tells the story of two warriors, the stablemates, and
how one of them wins a girl who is playing hard to get. Despite all
that she does to put them off, they persevere, and eventually the
maiden is swayed by her suitor's winning words.

One evening out on Doverfell,
  Two warriors sat and drank their fill.
And we should carry the runes so well,
  With honour.

Stablemate spoke to stablemate there:
  "Will you not ride away to get married this year?"

"I know of no maiden here in the land,
  "To whom I'd give my word and my hand."

"I will show you so fair a wife,
  "But if you ask her, it'll cost you your life."

"I will give you my palfrey grey,
  "If you, my stablemate, show me the way.

"I will give you my palfrey white,
    "If you, my stablemate, show me this sight."

When they had come to the rosy moors,
    They saw a wolf with a thigh in its jaws.

And stablemate spoke to stablemate then:
    "Let's turn around and ride home again."

"We've come so far up into the land,
    "So, my stablemate, let's carry on."

And when they had come to the miller's dam,
    They saw that the stream with red blood ran.

"Listen up, dear stablemate mine,
    "Tell me, what is this terrible sign?"

"This is all the knights' red blood,
    "Who came to court the maiden good."

And stablemate spoke to stablemate then:
    "Now we should turn and ride home again."

"We've come so far up into the land,
    "So, my stablemate, let's carry on."

And when the maiden's fence appeared,
    They saw that the stakes were made of spears.

On every stake in the fence that stood,
    Was set a man's head, covered in blood.

"Listen up, O stablemate mine,
    "Tell me, what is this terrible sign?"

"These are all the good knights' heads,
    "Who came the maiden fair to wed."

They saw that the stream with red blood ran.

And stablemate spoke to stablemate then:
"Now we should turn and ride home again."

"We've come so far up into the land,
"So, my stablemate, let's carry on."

And so they rode into the maiden's yard,
And there they found where the watchman stood.

"Watchman, watchman, let us in,
"I will give you my red-gold ring."

"Your red-gold ring is fair and fine,
"If only the maiden I dared to defy."

The maiden she looked through the window and said:
"Who is this stranger out in my yard?"

The maiden stood up and she brushed her hair,
She set on her head a golden crown rare.

The maiden she called over all her yard:
"Dress yourselves, guards, in iron so hard."

The maiden she called for iron and sword:
"Now give the same fate to this warrior lord!"

"My dear fair maiden, don't say that,
"For I am the young man who you should have."

"If you were the young man who I should take,
"Then you'd have brought gold on your palfrey's back."

"It's a part of warrior-lore,
"Leave the gold at home when you ride to war.

"It's a part of the warriors' way,
"When you ride to fight, the gold should stay."

The maiden she called to her small boys two:
"Now down to the cellar you should go.

"And fetch us up both mead and wine,
"For this man will be the dearest of mine."

And there was joy and great delight,
The warrior married the maiden that night.
And we should carry the runes so well,
With honour.

And there he met a travelling man.

7 | Sven Swan-White

This is an example of a riddle song. Several of the riddles have a Christian religious theme, while others are based on nature.

Sven Swan-White he rode the road along,
    And there he met a travelling man:
"Traveller, hear what I say to you:
    "Can you answer the riddles I ask of you?"

"No riddles have I ever read,
    "But I beat the King of Iceland dead."
"If you beat the King of Iceland dead,
    "Then that was my father you beat to death."

Sven Swan-White he hit the man with his thumb,
    So out of him flew his liver and lungs.
Sven Swan-White he beat him to pieces so small,
    Like leaves to the ground in autumn fall.

Sven Swan-White along the road went on,
    And he met another travelling man:
"Traveller, hear what I say to you:
    "Can you answer the riddles I ask of you?"

"What is it that's rounder than a wheel?
"And where can you find the fairest deer?
"And where does the sun go to its seat?
"And where does a dead man put his feet?"

"The sun is rounder than a wheel,
"In heaven there are the fairest deer,
"In the west the sun goes to its seat,
"In the east a dead man has his feet."

"What is blacker still than coal?
"And what is quicker than lark-wings small?
"What is whiter than a swan?
"And what calls louder than a crane?"

"Sin is blacker still than coal,
"The soul is quicker than lark-wings small,
"An angel's whiter than a swan,
"And thunder's louder than a crane."

"What's the broadest bridge you know?
"And what goes fastest against the flow?
"And where does the way lead that is smoothest?
"And where does the man lie who is cruelest?"

"Ice builds the broadest bridge I know,
"And fish swim fastest against the flow,
"The way to hell it is the smoothest,
"And there the man lies who is cruelest."

They drank for days, they drank for four,
"If you know all those things, you must know more."
Sven Swan-White he took the rings from his hand,
And he gave them all to the travelling man.

8   The Cloister Raid

This ballad tells the story of events around the time of the foundation of the Swedish state in the 1200s, when Sune Folkesson stole away Helena Sverkersdotter (the daughter of King Sverker) from the convent at Vreta. While it is known that Helena Sverkersdotter was in Vreta convent, and that she did marry Sune Folkesson, historical documentation of further detail of the story is sparse. Sune Folkesson and Elin (i.e., Helena), the main subjects of the ballad, can be readily identified, along with one of their daughters, Karin (i.e., Katarina). However, the other characters in the ballad, King Magnus, sister Karin, brother Knut, and daughters Kerstin and Adelin, do not have the same names as historical figures.

In the ballad, Sune Folkesson and his brother Knut break into the convent at Vreta, and having killed her guards, they brutally carry off Miss Elin, the daughter of King Magnus of Sweden, half-dressed from her bed, to Sune's estate at Ymseborough. Elin had had dreams that gave her signs that this fate awaited her. The Folkesson men had waited until her father, the King, was dead before they carried out the raid. It is clear that Elin was not carried away willingly, nor happily married to Sune, who continued to treat her very badly. At the end of the ballad, as she lies dying, Elin speaks to her three daughters borne during her years of marriage to Sune. She tells one of her daughters, Adelin, that she should go into the convent, and she dies without forgiving Sune for all his maltreatment of her.

In fact, one of Helena Sverkersdotter's daughters with Sune Folkesson, Benedicta, did go into Vreta convent, and she too was carried off, in this case by Lars Petterson. Even Benedicta's daughter, Ingrid, was taken from the same convent by Folke Algotsson. The ballads *Junker Lars's Cloister Raid* and *Folke Algotsson's Bride Raid* tell of these events.

The heroes they lie beaten,
   So wide in Sweden's land,
All since Sir Sune Folkesson,
   He stole that maiden's hand.
There lie the heroes beaten.

There was great distress in Sweden,
   And anger all around,
All since the men of the Folkunga clan,
   Broke Vreta Cloister down.

King Magnus he ruled in Sweden,
   Both rich and brave was he,
So pretty were his daughters two,
   The fairest you could see.

King Magnus he held a council,
   And the elders counselled so:
Miss Elin should go to Vreta Cloister,
   And Miss Karin the land should rule.

It was Sir Sune Folkesson,
   He spoke to his brother Knut:
"To Vreta Cloister we will ride,
"To take Miss Elin out!"

"If we ride to Vreta Cloister,
  "And with the maiden fly,
"If her father, King Magnus, hears of it,
  "Then we will surely die."

It was the men of the Folkunga clan,
  For saddle and horse they called:
"Now we will ride to Uppsala,
  "And on King Magnus call."

And so they rode to Uppsala,
  To the castle they went in.
They asked after King Magnus,
  But it wasn't good for him.

Out came a little court-boy,
  Clad in a shirt so grey:
"King Magnus he lies in the high loft,
  "So long so ill he's lain."

And so it was King Magnus,
  He died that very night,
And quickly came the tidings out,
  To greet the noble knights.

It was Sir Sune Folkesson,
  For saddle and horse he called:
"To Vreta Cloister we will ride,
  "And on the rich maiden call.

"If we ride to Vreta Cloister,
  "And there a wife we win,
"You may know, my brother Knut,
  "That maiden will be mine."

Miss Elin had a dream that night,
  Asleep she lay in bed.
By early morning she awoke,
  And to the abbess said:

"I dreamed my father's falcons,
  "They were no more than three.
"They sat there on our cloister-roof,
  "And called so pitifully.

"I dreamed my father's falcons,
  "That to the east they flew.
"I fear that sorrow will fill my breast,
  "I've lately feared it true.

"I dreamed of the soaring eagle,
  "And also the flying raven.
"They started a fight between themselves,
  "And into my arms they came."

And so it was the abbess,
  The dreams she'd reason through:
"It is the men of the Folkunga clan,
  "Often they think of you.

"Did you dream your father's falcons,
  "They were no more than three?
"It is Sir Sune Folkesson,
  "He'll bring you sorrow and grief.

"Did you dream your father's falcons,
  "That to the east they flew?
"It is Sir Sune Folkesson,
  "Daily he thinks of you.

"Did you dream of the soaring eagle,
   "And also the flying raven?
"It is Sir Sune Folkesson,
   "He'll bring you sorrow and pain."

Seven times then the noblemen,
   The cloister rode around.
They stopped before the cloister-wall,
   And began to break it down.

Out came a little cloister-maid,
   Clad in a shirt so green:
"Who is breaking our cloister-wall,
   "And making such a din?"

"Listen, little cloister-maid,
   "To what I say to you:
"Tell me where Miss Elin sleeps,
   "Don't hide it from me now!"

"The house is built of marble-stone,
   "The roof it is of lead,
"And covered all with silken sheets,
   "There is the maiden's bed."

And then awoke the abbess,
   She called her handmaids in:
"Who is breaking our cloister-wall,
   "And who will come herein?"

"Sir Knut he breaks the cloister-wall,
   "Sir Sune he'll come in,
"Sir Sune will put out the candle-light,
   "That burns for Miss Elin."

Seven times then the noblemen the cloister rode around.

And then awoke the maiden's knight,
  He spoke to his brother so:
"And we must offer our young lives,
  "For our dear mistress now."

Nor could the men of the Folkunga clan,
  Take Miss Elin away,
Until they'd beaten her twelve knights,
  So dead at her feet they lay.

Bare-headed then, and barefoot,
  They carried her from the door,
And never was a royal maid,
  So pitifully borne.

And so they cast a cape of blue,
  Over her yellow hair,
And lifted her onto a palfrey grey,
  And took her away from there.

They rode away all through the day,
  Away from Vreta's land.
"Listen up, Miss Elin fair,
  "You give my brother your hand!"

"Be quiet, Sir Knut Folkesson,
  "Don't say such things to me.
"For I have often sworn before,
  "Sir Sune will never have me."

And it was fair Miss Elin,
  She spoke so to herself:
"When my father, King Magnus, hears of this,
  "Then he must surely help."

It was Sir Sune Folkesson,
  Her sorrow he made clear:
"King Magnus he lies in the high loft,
"All on a gilded bier."

"If what you say to me is true,
  "King Magnus my father's dead,
"Then there is no-one in the world,
  "To save me in my distress."

It was Sir Sune Folkesson,
  He took her to Ymseborough.
And this I say to you in truth,
  She lived in daily sorrow.

They lived together fifteen years,
  They lived together so,
And neither to the other gladly said,
  Even "yes" or "no"!

'Twas on a Wednesday evening,
  Miss Elin held her side.
She prayed to God so earnestly,
  Her time would soon arrive.

And it was fair Miss Elin,
  She spoke to her handmaids two:
"Go and ask Sir Sune Folkesson,
  "To come here to my room."

In then stepped her handmaids two,
  Clad in shirts so red:
"Sir Sune, go to Miss Elin now,
  "I fear she'll soon be dead."

In came Sir Sune Folkesson,
   All wrapped in a scarlet skin:
"Why have you called me so urgently,
   "Away from those guests of mine?"

"I have a great pain in my side,
   "I hope I'll soon be dead.
"I thank our heavenly father God,
   "Who frees me from my distress."

It was Sir Sune Folkesson,
   He patted her on the cheek:
"Forgive me all I've done you wrong,
   "All-dearest, I beseech."

"You'll never be forgiven,
   "For all you've done me harm,
"For when you took my serving girl,
   "And laid her on your arm.

"Yes you took my serving girl,
   "And lay on the pillows of blue,
"But me you've pulled me by my hair,
   "And cursed and beaten too."

It was Sir Sune Folkesson,
   He stroked her flower-cheek:
"Forgive me all I've done you wrong,
   "All-dearest, I beseech."

"You'll never be forgiven,
   "For all my misery.
"Seven daughters have I had with you,
   "Who I may never see.

"Seven daughters have I had with you,
  "All with so much pain.
"Four maidens they've already died,
  "The other three remain."

So soon was spread the silk of red,
  And velvet fair and fine,
And forth were led the maidens three,
  Before their mother in.

"Welcome here Miss Karin,
  "Eldest daughter of mine.
"Welcome here Miss Kerstin,
  "The King of Spain's fair bride.

"And welcome too Miss Adelin,
  "My youngest daughter here,
"You'll go into Vreta Cloister,
  "And follow your mother dear."

And so it was Miss Adelin,
  The tears on her cheeks ran:
"I'll never go into the cloister,
  "I'd rather marry a man."

And it was fair Miss Elin,
  She wrung her hands distraught:
"So shall my words still not be heard,
  "Even by my daughters?"

And so it was Miss Adelin,
  Her cheeks were wet with tears:
"Of course I'll go into the cloister,
  "By your will, O mother dear."

"To the cloister I was given,
  "With but a silken shirt,
"And from there I was taken,
  "So much my heart it hurt."

It was Sir Sune Folkesson,
  The tears fell on his cheeks:
"Forgive me all I've done you wrong,
  "All-dearest, I beseech."

"So put away your scarlet skin,
  "Tear up your cape so blue,
"For the days you had a royal bride,
  "Are over now for you."

And it was fair Miss Elin,
  She turned her face away,
And this I say to you in truth,
  She died that very day.

It was Sir Sune Folkesson,
  He buried her in state,
And so he had her burial-chest,
  With gilded letters laid.
  There lie the heroes beaten.

Until he came to the mountain blue, and saw the smoke and sparks.

9 | Heming and the Mountain Troll

This ballad and the next one both tell stories of Heming the young, an expert skier. In this first ballad, he has a run-in with a mountain troll (who is sometimes referred to as a troll-mother or an old woman in the ballad). She has taken Heming's girl away to her home in the mountains. When Heming eventually finds them, he promises to remain there (as the troll requests), but as soon as she goes out, Heming flees with the girl. The ballad ends when the troll, by then in hot pursuit, is turned to stone at the sight of a Christian symbol — the cross.

> The first child that Norcka bore,
>   He lived high in the fell.
> He learned to hunt the hart and deer,
>   And learned to ski so well.
> *Heming the young he could run on his skis so well.*

> Now Heming loved a maiden,
>   He missed her very much.
> A troll-mother stole her from the church,
>   All in a dreadful rush.

The spring-time it was coming,
    And farmers drove the plough,
But Heming left his oxen there,
    And wondered where he'd go.

Heming searched the forest far,
    He found a great white bear,
Where she lay and fed her cubs,
    All in her winter lair.

He drew his bow against his foot,
    He shot her in the side:
"With this you shouldn't feel as good,
    "As when your cubs you fed."

Up then rose the great white bear,
    She slapped him with her paws:
"And neither should you feel as good,
    "As when your girl you saw."

Heming searched still further on,
    Along the water-mark,
Until he came to the mountain blue,
    And saw the smoke and sparks.

And Heming went into the mountain,
    From where the smoke rose higher,
And there he found the troll-mother,
    Who poked with her nose in the fire.

"Where've you come from, spoilt brat?
    "You've come so very late,
"Either you would have some fire,
    "Or lodging for the night."

54

"I am not a spoilt brat!
"You shouldn't call me this,
"And now I've come to the mountain high,
"To find the maid I've missed.

"Listen, old woman, what I say to you,
"One thing you'll give to me:
"I would have your reddest gold,
"And the maiden where she sleeps."

"Of course you'll have my reddest gold,
"And the maiden where she lies,
"If you will only give your word,
"To live in the mountain high."

"Of course I'll let you have my word,
"We'll stay in the mountain high,
"If I could see your reddest gold,
"And the maiden where she lies."

The old woman put on a coat of fur,
    She didn't want to freeze,
And she left to run all round the land,
    The wedding-fayre to choose.

And Heming took the maiden out,
    They had to ski away.
She fell in a faint his fair young maid,
    When the mountain shook and swayed.

So Heming took some powder snow,
    To rub her forehead there.
She came to life his fair young wife,
    And Heming smiled at her.

The old woman came to the mountain blue,
  She searched but all in vain:
For gone was all her reddest gold,
  And the maiden where she'd lain.

The old woman ran from the mountain blue,
  Across the sunless heath,
And where the trees in the forest grew,
  She stooped to come beneath.

And it was Heming the young,
  He came to the salty sound.
The troll-mother she ran behind,
  Her tongue hung down on the ground.

And soon they came to the long bridge,
  She saw the cross too late:
"Lord God have mercy, my fair young swain,
  "You save me from my fate!"

The old woman came to the long bridge,
  She saw the cross above her.
She shattered into blocks of stone,
  And Heming's cares were over.

"Listen, Heming, what I say to you,
  "One thing you'll do I pray:
"Help me back to the mountain blue,
  "So I here mustn't stay."

"Listen, old woman, what I say to you,
  "In your grimy gown:
"You're worth no better than to lie,
  "As milestones on the ground."
Heming the young he could run on his skis so well.

56

10   Heming and King Harald

This Norwegian ballad tells the story of the sporting contests of Heming the young (a son of Aslack) with King Harald Hardrada. The ballad begins similarly to *Widrick Waylandsson's Fight with Long-Ben Reyser*: Here, King Harald is reflecting on his great prowess, and it is suggested to him that Heming might be his match. Harald sails away to find Heming, and the two of them compete at archery and skiing. In the initial archery competition, conventional target shooting, nothing can separate the two. Harald then challenges Heming to some very difficult or impossible tasks, and he either achieves these or makes his own impossible challenges in return. He shoots a nut placed on top of his brother's head, and skis impressively down Snarafell. The name of the mountain Snarafell is significant — *snara* means quick, and so the fell is presumably difficult and dangerous to ski on, and it also means trap (*cf* English *snare*). But Heming is not caught in Harald's trap, and in fact, Heming kills Harald at the end of the song.

The story of Heming and Harald Hardrada is also told in the Icelandic Flatey book manuscript as *The Story of Heming Aslacksson*, and in a Færoese ballad called *Geyti Aslacksson*. Both of these versions tell of further elements that are not included in this song, including a swimming competition, and the stealing of the King's knife. Other very similar folk-tales are known: the Danish hero Palna-Toki is said to have had a similar archery and skiing encounter with another familiar King Harald, Harald Bluetooth, at Kullaberg in Skåne; English tradition tells of William of Cloudsley, who was forced to shoot an apple from his son's head in the Inglewood forest south of Carlisle.

King Harald he sat on the broad bench,
    Was speaking to his band:
"I fear I cannot find my match,
    "In these earthly lands."
Heming the young he could run on his skis so well.

King Harald he sat on the broad bench,
    Was speaking to his men:
"I say I cannot find my match,
    "He mustn't yet be born."

A little small boy answered,
    Was standing close at heel:
"I know of a strong fighter who,
    "Wrings water out of steel.

"And even the horse of Heming,
    "When you meet it on the road,
"It's like a dragon in its eyes,
    "And fire flares from its nose."

And it was Harald the King,
    Before their noses paced:
"If I live a day beyond tonight,
    "That fighter I shall face."

So they hoisted high the silken sails,
    Upon the gilded masts,
And didn't let those sails be struck,
    Till Aslack's land they passed.

I see so many Orlock ships, sailing into land.

King Aslack he stood in the high loft,
    He looked out over the strand:
"I see so many Orlock ships,
    "Sailing into land.

"Now stay inside, O son of mine,
    "And with the maids drink mead,
"While I go down all to the strand,
    "To see who they might be."

And so it was King Aslack,
    He went down to the strand.
And so it was King Harald,
    He steered his ship to land.

And so it was King Harald,
    The first who stepped ashore:
"Listen, old man in the field,
    "Your real name I'll hear."

"I'll let you know my real name,
    "If you would have it done:
"Aslack the King I am called,
    "And Heming's my youngest son."

And it was Heming the young,
    He thought there was no threat.
He saddled up his fleet-foot foal,
    And to the strand he went.

"God protect you, son of mine,
    "Why didn't you stay inside?
"You should be shy or take more care,
    "It's better for you to hide."

"Listen up, O father dear,
"Don't worry about that.
"I haven't had my fingers hurt,
"Big battles I've been at.

"Listen up, O father dear,
"Don't worry about me.
"My childhood I have left behind,
"My horse I've ridden here."

"I hear you Heming the young,
"With me you want to fight.
"So meet me out on the gamesfield,
"When the sunshine reddens the heights."

'Twas early in the morning,
The sun shone red on the heights.
And all young Heming longed for was,
To ride his horse to the fight.

'Twas early in the morning,
The sun shone red on the fell.
The arrows all hit their target-marks,
Like stars from the skies they fell.

'Twas early in the morning,
The sun shone red on the tops.
And neither one could the other beat.
Their arrow-heads touched at the tips.

"I hear you Heming the young,
"You always will succeed,
"So you shall shoot a walnut,
"Upon your brother's head."

"Yes I shall shoot a walnut,
"Upon my brother's head,
"And you, O King, shall stand beside,
"And watch me do the deed."

"Listen my dear brother,
"Don't stand so pale and blue,
"But stand under the walnut,
"And stand both straight and true."

And it was Heming the young,
He made a direct hit.
One piece down to his shoulder fell,
Lay still the second bit.

King Harald he spoke to Heming:
"The challenge now is over.
"But why do you have another arrow,
"Hidden in your quiver?"

"Had I shot my brother,
"Had things gone quite so badly,
"This shining arrow would have flown,
"Through you, Harald, gladly."

"I hear you Heming the young,
"You never will return,
"You shall find that man for me,
"For friends he hasn't one."

"If I bring that man to you,
"For friends he hasn't one,
"Then you shall light the running beck,
"All so it starts to burn."

"I hear you Heming the young,
  "It seems you have no fear,
"You shall ski out on the fell,
  "The one the boys call Snara."

"Yes I shall ski out on the fell,
  "The one the boys call Snara,
"And you, O King, shall stand below,
  "All so your view is clearer."

Heming skied on Snarafell,
  His skis they turned on high.
The King he thought he seemed to see,
  The stars falling out of the sky.

Heming skied on Snarafell,
  His skis they ran on the snow.
He took the King by the shoulder-bone,
  So his nose hit the earth below.

And it was Heming the young,
  He turned around his course:
"And if you've had too little still,
  "Then I have plenty more."

And so he cut off Harald's hand,
  And both his shoulder-bones.
The King's men were more bothered by,
  The snow upon his clothes.

Heming he put on his oaken skis,
  He skied off north to the fells,
And everyone asked but no-one knew,
  Where that young man did dwell.

Heming he ran on his oaken skis,
   He skied to the hills so high,
And everyone asked but no-one knew,
   How that young man would die.
Heming the young he could run on his skis so well.

Notes

I have primarily used the ballads transcribed in *Svenska Forn-sånger*, 1834–1842, by A. I. Arwidsson (*A*), and *Svenska Folkvi-sor Från Forntiden*, 1814–1816, by E. G. Geijer and A. A. Afzelius (*GA*) as the starting point for the English versions presented here. These are occasionally supplemented with sources from elsewhere in the Scandinavian tradition, i.e., *Danmarks Gamle Folkeviser*, 1853–1904, by S. Grundtvig (*G*), and the online *Ballad Archive of the Norwegian Dokumentasjonsprosjektet* (*N*).

Widrick Waylandsson's Fight with Long-Ben Reyser – My version most closely follows *Widrik Werlandsons Kamp med Hög-ben Rese* (*A*3A), but with several verses from *A*3B and *A*3C, and from the Danish *Kong Diderik og hans Kæmper* (*G*7A).

Twelve Strong Fighters – My version most closely follows *De Tolf Starke Kämpar* (*A*4A), but with some verses from *A*4B and *A*4C, and some lines from the Danish *Kong Diderik og hans Kæmper* (*G*7A).

Hilla-Lill – My version closely follows *Stolts Hilla* (*GA*32), but with some verses from *Hilla Lillas Klagan* (*A*107) and from the Danish *Hildebrand og Hilde* (*G*83A).

Sir Hjalmar – My version closely follows *Herr Hjälmer* (*A*21), with some verses from *Herr Helmer* (*GA*54A and B).

The Hammer Hunt – My version is based on *Hammarhämtningen* (*A*1), but some verses are taken from versions of the Norwegian *Torekall* (*N*).

The Stablemates – My version closely follows *Stallbroderna* (*A*113), but with some verses from the Danish *Den Farlige Jumfrun* (*G*184), and also from a second Swedish version given under *G*184.

Sven Swan-White – Sven Swan-White was printed and widely distributed, so it is well known with few variations. For example, *Sven Svanehvit* is found as *GA*45.

The Cloister Raid – My version is essentially based on *Wreta Kloster-rof* (*A*163), but with some lines from *Klosterrovet* (*GA*27).

Heming and the Mountain Troll – My version is essentially based on *Bergtrollet* (*A*13), but with some lines from the Norwegian *Hemingen og Gygri* (*N*).

Heming and King Harald – From versions of the Norwegian *Hemingen og Harald Kongen* (*N*).